The Story of a Warrior Who Broke Free from Mental Anguish

A MEMOIR

LeShawn Fernandez

The Story of a Warrior Who Broke Free from Mental Anguish

A MEMOIR

LeShawn Fernandez

ARPress
45 Dan Road Suite 15
Canton MA 02021

Hotline:	1(888) 821-0229
Fax:	1(508) 545-7580

Ordering Information:
Quantity sales. Special discounts are available on quantity purchases by corporations, associations, and others. For details, contact the publisher at the address above.

Printed in the United States of America.

ISBN-13:	Softcover	979-8-89676-667-4
	eBook	979-8-89676-668-1

Library of Congress Control Number: 2026906444

Contents

Dedication

I dedicate this book to my birth mother, Josephine Hagger, a woman of strength who endured great pain, even when I could not help. The memories I have of you will always hold a special place in my heart.

To John Edward Sr., my adoptive Daddy, thank you for giving me a childhood filled with experiences I will always cherish.

To Maybelle Edwards, my adoptive Mom, thank you for encouraging me to take that licensing exam, it made all the difference—I PASSED and I am doing great in the insurance field.

May you all continue to REST IN PEACE.

Acknowledgments

I would first like to acknowledge my oldest daughter, **Ingrid Fernandez**. I had you so young, we practically grew up together. You inspired me to slow down when I could and smell the roses. You are the one who learned your controlling ways from me before I healed. That mouth was savage! However, through trial and error, raising you taught me how to be a mother. I love you!

To my youngest daughter, **Mariah Toussaint**, you were headstrong and mirrored me. You caused me to see many of my self-sabotaging behaviors. That savage mouth that you learned from my behavior, taught me to think before I speak. I love you!

To my middle child, **Miracle Toussaint**, thank you for your humble spirit and for leading and guiding in love, to do what makes one happy... just as you have taught me.

To **Katheryn M**, my college professor at Kennesaw State, thank you for staying back with me every day and for tutoring me because I struggled with English, being from New Orleans, LA. You were patient with me. I appreciate you for never giving up on me and even teaching me outside of your work schedule.

To **Lecritia M**—my best friend Nay, for over 35 years. Thank you for all you have done for me over the years. Your role as my girl's personal nanny gave me the opportunity to conquer the dreams and goals I wanted to achieve and make decent money.

Tameka B—another best friend for nearly 30 years. Thank you for opening the door to my dream of being a daycare owner by allowing me to babysit your kids and telling other parents about me so they would bring their kids too.

Finally, to my King, **Richard W**—the first man to respect me and show me genuine love even when I sabotaged the relationship many times. Thank you for never giving up on me and for giving me time and space when I needed it. Your love for me has allowed me to sit down and stop running from the problem, which was myself. With my unhealed mindset and insecurities from childhood; your wisdom and knowledge has allowed me to be a student.

As the saying goes, the teacher will appear when the student is ready. Your divine, genuine love took me out of living in my masculinity to operating in my femininity, my soft girl era, something I never did. I learned how to survive by being in my masculine role. Now, because of you, I have mastered how to balance the two. So, when they say the man changes for the right woman. I agree, I also believe the same happened when the Divine God Himself sent my king into my life. This man's support, prayers, encouragement, and breathing life into me helped this queen heal.

I transformed, and now I am a new creature. Old ways are gone, and all things are new! 2 Corinthians 5:17

The truth is all my girls are my redeeming qualities. Each one molded me differently to be the best mother I could be when I never had the guidance and love I needed. I love my daughters and grandkids as they are my beacons of light.

Finally, **my Heavenly Father, the Divine, The Great I am, The beginning, The end, The Alpha, The Omega, my all**. I can go on and on now since I have a personal relationship with God now. This joy, this peace the world did not give it, and the world cannot take it away. God carried me through the years I was lost, broken into a million pieces. He was the Potter, and I was the clay. He put me back together better than my original state.

This spiritual journey was not easy, but it was worth it. This walk is not for the faint at heart. I failed several times to heal, and God did not force me. He waited patiently, awaiting me with open arms like the Prodigal son, and after two years, almost three, I told God I was ready and would say yes to His will. I was done doing it my way. I am so thankful I did. My life is complete because I healed and love me wholeheartedly. But having God dwell in me is a fantastic feeling I cannot explain sometimes.

Thank you for supporting me by purchasing and reading my book. I hope it blesses you as much as I enjoyed sharing my journey and how I made it over! Now, do not forget the homework. Complete the assignments in the workbook and journal to help you heal on this incredible journey you are about to embark on.

Introduction

Dear Beautiful Souls

With a heart overflowing with gratitude and trembling with anticipation, I'm honored to finally share something that has lived in the quiet corners of my spirit for years—a project born from both pain and purpose. "The Story of a Warrior...Who Broke Free From Mental Anguish" is not just a book—it's a lifeline, a love letter to the wounded heart, and a testimony to the strength that rises from broken places.

This story has been pressing on my heart, whispering to be told. It's the raw, unfiltered truth of my life—a medley of moments marked by deep loss, unexpected love, and the persistent search for identity and belonging. Through these pages, I open the door to my soul, inviting you to walk with me through the shadows and into the light.

The Story of a Warrior is more than a personal memoir—it's a blessed offering—a reflection of what it means to survive the things meant to break us. To sit in the ache of unanswered questions and still rise. To love, to lose, and to somehow find ourselves again—sometimes in pieces, always in truth.

Healing is not a straight line. It's messy, it's painful, and it's beautifully brave. It demands that we face our past with trembling hands and an open heart. And yet, in that sacred space, change is born. This book is both a mirror and a map—a companion for anyone walking through grief, wrestling with identity, or searching for a deeper sense of self.

If you've ever felt unseen

If you've ever questioned your worth

If you've ever longed to feel whole again—this is for you.

Through my tears, triumphs, and truth, I pray this story becomes a soft place to land for those who need hope. Let it be your reminder that healing is possible and you are never alone.

I would love for you to walk this journey with me—not just in the pages of this book, but in the community. Join me on social media, where I share heartfelt reflections, glimpses into the healing process, and moments of grace. Let's build a space together—where scars are honored, stories are shared, and souls are reminded they still matter.

From the bottom of my heart, thank you for allowing me to share my truth. May it speak to the tender places within you and ignite your journey toward healing.

With love, vulnerability, and deep gratitude,

Leshawn Fernandez

Chapter One

When the Pain Begins

1974. I was born into a family marked by both love and turmoil. Shadows shaped my earliest years, which I didn't yet understand. My father, a man whose name I never knew, remains a mystery to this day. My mother, Josephine Hagger, gave me life and love, and it wasn't until I turned twelve that I learned her name, which I had discovered on a worn birth certificate just before her name was struck from my legal records as if she had never existed.

We made our home in the heart of New Orleans, rooted in the city's rich culture and its struggles. I grew up beside my younger sister, Lekisha, born in 1977, and my brother, Michael, born in 1979. But I've never known how my parents met or what brought them together. In our world, asking such questions was taboo, disrespectful, even. You didn't question your parents; you just learned to survive them.

My mother, despite everything, was a present and loving force in our lives. She was my protector, especially from my father's unpredictable temper. I remember how we would both tense at the sound of his footsteps. Sometimes, it didn't take a reason for his rage to erupt, it just came. We moved through our days like programmed machines, adhering to routines that made life bearable, if not peaceful.

The most unimaginable things could set off his anger. And when he exploded, it was terrifying. I can still hear his voice, coarse and angry, invading my dreams, jolting me awake in a sweat. I witnessed things no child should ever have to see. I watched my mother become a punching bag for his fury, his fists, his boots, her head against the wall. If I had the power back then, I would have begged her to run. But we were stuck, hostages in a home fueled by alcohol and fear.

Living in the projects, life came with its own set of challenges. We faced economic hardship, scarce resources, and the constant threat of violence. I often felt the pressure of being the eldest, carrying responsibilities that were too heavy for my young shoulders. I remember curling up behind my bedroom door, hiding from the chaos outside, praying for silence. The violence wasn't just something we witnessed—it was something we breathed in daily.

Despite the pain, I saw my mother's strength. I also saw her breaking. Her body grew weaker with time, and slowly, I began to notice strangers—men and women in white coats—coming to take her away. I didn't understand at the time, but later, I realized they were admitting her to a mental health facility. That truth hit me hard. I felt helpless—wishing I had known more, been older, stronger, wiser. I wanted to protect her, but I was still just a girl.

And then, one day, she was gone and gone forever.

That was the first deep crack in the foundation of my world. The second came years later when my brother Michael was taken from us—killed at the age of thirtyone. The circumstances around his death were never fully explained. The unanswered questions only deepened the wounds.

Even amid all this loss, the most complex grief I carried was the one tied to my father. As a young girl, I yearned for his attention. I would watch other kids talk about fishing trips with their dads, laughter-filled afternoons, and hugs before bedtime. I wanted that so badly. I used to stand silently by the door, hoping he would notice me. But he never did—not through the fog of his drinking, not through the haze of his anger.

And yet, somehow, I was still "Daddy's little girl." My mother often sent me to the bar to fetch him, too afraid to face his public scorn. I walked into smoky rooms filled with loud voices and heavy air, hoping I could coax him home. It wasn't love—it was survival masquerading as devotion. I didn't get the affection I craved, but I learned how to exist in its absence.

In those years, my bedroom became my refuge—a world of drawings and daydreams where I imagined a different kind of family. One with peace. One with love. One with a father who danced with his daughter instead of drowning in silence and whiskey.

The scars from that time didn't just fade. They shaped the way I understood love, relationships, and myself. I carried a deep longing into every connection, always searching for the validation I never received at home. There was always something missing, always a part of me that felt incomplete.

But through all of it—the trauma, the losses, the silence, and the screams—I survived.

Growing up in the projects of New Orleans taught me how to navigate pain, stand in my truth, and fight for healing. It shaped my voice and my mission. It gave me the strength to turn my story into something more than sorrow—it became a testimony. A lesson in resilience. A call to others who have walked through darkness and are still searching for the light.

This is more than a memoir—it's my soul on paper. A tribute to my mother, a love letter to my younger self, and a reminder to anyone reading: you are not alone.

With every word I write, I take one step closer to wholeness. And I hope, as you walk this journey with me, you'll feel more seen, a little more understood, and a whole lot more hopeful.

Chapter Two

Choice-less

My earliest memories are shrouded in a haze of confusion and an overwhelming sense of loss. At just five years old, I faced a life-altering change that I could not comprehend at that time. The state took my siblings and me and placed us in foster homes. My mother, being in a mental institution and unable to care for us due to her struggles with mental health, made the painful decision to place us in the foster care system. It was not my choice, and neither could I influence any change. We were separated and put into different foster homes.

At the age of five, I was placed with a foster family that had already opened their home to five teenage boys, ranging in age from fourteen to sixteen. My foster mother, who was a nurse, worked all the time, so it seemed like she was rarely home.

The reality of living there quickly became a nightmare. What happened within those walls was a dark secret I was threatened to keep, no matter what. I was raped repeatedly by the five boys and my foster father. The molestation and assaults were relentless and lasted from the time I entered their home at age five until I was seven. As I relive that time in my life, I can't believe the foster care system allowed a five-year-old girl to be placed in a home where there were already five boys. To keep me compliant and silent, they threatened me, made me feel like I was the problem, and ensured I stayed quiet even at school. "You better not say a word to anyone" was their favorite phrase.

Starvation was another tool they used to control me. I went to bed every night hungry. That was the punishment for being a "bad child," as my foster father would tell his wife.

My foster mother, while she should have been protecting me, turned a blind eye and a deaf ear. As a nurse, especially, she should have been able to see beyond my quietness and see that something was wrong. She was supposed to be the mother figure, but instead of noticing the difference in the way I walked and how I groaned in pain, she chose to accept her husband's false claims that I was a "bad" child and refused to feed me as punishment. I would go to bed hungry every night. I always looked forward to school not for learning but because it meant I would get something to eat.

As I said, every decision in my life was made by someone else. "I was choiceless." The government placed me in foster care when I was too young to consent; my innocence was forcefully taken from me. My virginity was taken in the most degrading, humiliating, and undignified way ever. I was demeaned, bruised, and treated like a piece of trash. What sort of sexual gratification could I give as a five-year-old? They did not care. "Spread your legs!" "You better not scream!" and "Lay back down!" was the constant song of my molesters—the desperate echo of man's cruelty.

At school, my teachers would tell my foster mother how well I was doing—excelling and reading above my grade level. But that did not matter to her; all that mattered was what her husband told her, which kept the abuse going.

I remember meeting the foster mother's sister once, who took me along with her little girl about the same age as me for a day out. It was the most fun I had in a long time, and I forgot about my reality for a moment. I felt like I was just released from the house of pain. I had a great time riding different rides and seeing other kids happy, too. I wished it were my reality. The genuine smiles on the other little girls' faces made me long for the true love of my parents. Getting back home, my foster mother's sister jokingly said I did not want to come back home because I had so much fun; my foster mother did not find that funny and quickly put an end to me going out with her sister or even seeing them. I never saw her sister or niece again. For the next two years, life was filled with nothing but sexual abuse, neglect, and the constant threat of punishment.

I often went to school on an empty stomach, suffering from pain in my legs and lower body. I appeared frail and disinterested in activities; some teachers thought I was a rebellious girl, while others considered me intelligent but vengeful. However, I was haunted by the warnings of my abusers echoing in my mind. My heart felt heavy, but I dared not speak about it. I was just a little girl carrying a heavy burden. The abuse continued, and my pain lingered. I told myself this was my fate—to be just an ordinary girl who would never be treasured.

My foster mom dedicated herself wholeheartedly to her work as a nurse, often working a significant amount of overtime. Unfortunately, her commitment and compassion for her job were void at home. She lacked affection or sympathy for anyone outside her professional duties. Each night, after long shifts at the hospital, she would come home, barely engaging with the family, and once she went to bed, she would fall into a deep sleep, rarely stirring until morning. There was no warmth or real connection in the household. I occupied a small room that was tucked away between the boys' room and my foster parents' room.

Nighttime filled me with dread; the sound of approaching footsteps sent chills down my spine. I would curl up in bed with nowhere to run, feeling small and vulnerable. In those moments, I trembled, fully aware of what was to come. They violated not only my body but my trust, with each of my foster brothers taking turns with me and leaving me trapped and powerless in a nightmare I could not escape from. I was completely shattered when my foster father, who should have also been protecting me, joined the boys in raping me. I was too young to understand what a miracle meant; all I knew was that I needed someone to save me. I was seven years old and already experiencing the worst pain and suffering of my life. I was living in pain, hunger, and abuse, and I had had enough. I may not have known what a miracle meant, but I understood what freedom meant and wanted to be free from this torment.

Chapter Three

Dealing With Two Faces of Abuse

After two long years in foster care, I was finally adopted by the Fernandez family at the age of seven. The feeling that washed over me was indescribable—a fragile mix of relief, hope, and fear. For the first time in what felt like forever, I had a place to call home.

My adoptive mother, Maybelle, initially showed interest only in my baby brother, Michael. He was just four months old at the time—small, helpless, and wrapped in a narrative that cast him as the cause of our biological mother's death. Rumors swirled around him like a storm, painting him as a tragedy in the making. People whispered that our mother had died giving birth to him, and that lie shaped how the world viewed us.

But the truth was far more painful and far less dramatic. Our mother didn't die in the delivery room—she passed away a few months after bringing Michael into the world. Her death wasn't immediate, but it was still devastating. That quiet truth got buried beneath gossip and blame, leaving behind a wound no one could see and few tried to understand.

That loss—and the shame and confusion it brought—ignited a fire in me. I wanted to belong. I wanted to feel whole in a world that had done nothing but tear me apart. So, when I stepped into my new home, I clung to hope. A hope that healing could begin and a hope that someone would finally see us—not as broken, but as worthy of love.

My adoptive father, John Edwards, was a dock worker who was away from home most of the time, working to provide for us. But though he wasn't always physically present, he was the quiet force that made our adoption possible. He was the one God used to bring us together. While Maybelle was focused on Michael, swayed by pity and public opinion, it was Father John's unwavering heart that changed the course of our lives. He saw past the rumors. He believed in keeping our family together. His compassion moved Maybelle to adopt not just Michael but all three of us—Michael, my sister Lekisha, and me.

Looking back, I can say this with truth in my bones: leaving foster care didn't erase the pain. The scars came with me. Life with my adoptive family was better, yes—but it was far from perfect. The abuse didn't end; it just took a different form. The sexual abuse I had known before was replaced with physical beatings, harsh words, and emotional torment.

And somewhere in all of that, I stopped being a child.

By the age of eight, I was no longer just a big sister—I was a caretaker. When my mother, Maybelle, gave birth to two more children, Erica and John, and my father was away working, my mother often helped my uncle run his business. The weight of responsibility fell squarely on my small shoulders. I was the one making sure everyone was fed, bathed, and looked after.

I was eight years old, and I was mothering four children.

I didn't know then that what I was doing was extraordinary. I only knew that it had to be done. I grew up too fast and lost my childhood before I even had a chance to live it.

But I survived. And in surviving, I began to write my story—one of pain, yes, but also of progress and, eventually, victory. The streets of New Orleans were both a danger and a strange sort of escape. Gunshots were a regular sound, echoing through our neighborhood like background music to our daily lives. Whenever I heard them ring out, I would immediately spring into action—pulling my siblings to the floor and covering them with my own body, using myself as a shield. What if I had gotten hit? What if one of those bullets had found me instead of missing? I asked myself that question more times than I could count.

Still, in the chaos, I tried to give us something resembling normalcy. We'd play outside when it felt safe, riding bikes and playing softball. Sometimes, I'd gather my siblings, and we'd "play church." I'd sneak chairs from the house and set up a makeshift congregation, preaching to them with all the authority I could muster. Even then, I was searching for comfort—reaching for hope in a world that rarely offered it.

In those moments, I found joy. Even when everything around me felt unsafe or uncertain, I had an imaginary Jesus who felt like my best friend. He was always with me—someone I could talk to, someone who understood what I couldn't put into words. My adoptive mother never knew about the sermons I delivered in our backyard, or how much those pretend services kept me grounded. It was my escape, my refuge, my peace.

For brief moments, I got to taste what childhood should feel like—simple, carefree. But those moments were fleeting. At home, my adoptive mother's words sliced through me like a knife. "You'll never amount to anything. The only thing you'll ever be good for is laying on your back." I was just a child, but those words left deep scars. I learned to endure them, just like I learned to endure the whippings—with belts, extension cords, and even a wooden bat.

As painful as it was, I told myself it was better than the foster home. At least here, I wasn't being molested. That was the trade-off. Physical and emotional abuse instead of sexual trauma. But it still broke something in me. It built up anger and resentment that I didn't know how to process.

Even so, my mother made sure we went to church. When my father was home, we'd attend a local parish together. That church became a sanctuary. Sundays quickly became my favorite day of the week—not because of the sermons or rituals, but because of the hope I felt when I walked through those doors.

Even when Daddy wasn't around, I'd walk to church with my siblings, excited to be in a place where I felt seen. I loved Sunday School. I loved learning about kindness and forgiveness, surrounded by kids who didn't look at me with pity or judgment. A few adults there made a point to talk to me—smiling warmly, calling me by name, making me feel like I mattered.

My adoptive mother, though, never joined us. She'd call it "Daddy's church," claiming that the people there were fake and full of gossip. When others asked her about our adoption, she'd fly into a rage. Eventually, she pulled us out altogether. Just like that, she took away the one place where I felt whole.

That church was where I had been baptized. I had dreamed of singing in the choir, joining youth programs, and being part of something good. But those dreams didn't matter to her. The minute it made her feel exposed or uncomfortable, it ended.

Even so, my belief in Jesus never left me. I talked to Him in my own way, sometimes unsure if I was doing it right—but always sure He was listening. In a life full of noise, He was my quiet place.

The church had been a refuge. A few hours a week where I didn't have to flinch, where I didn't have to hide bruises or silence my tears. But no matter how far I ran, the memories followed. The physical scars faded, but the emotional ones lingered. They still do.

And yet, somehow, I held on.

I kept breathing.

Kept hoping.

Kept surviving.

In my era, there were no school buses to take us back and forth. We walked—rain, shine, or cold winds. I have to give her credit, though. My adoptive mother ensured that I attended decent schools—better than the ones I could have easily ended up in. But getting there wasn't just a walk down the street. After dropping my siblings off at daycare, I had a long way to go to get to my school. Still, that walk felt like a small escape. For a little while, I didn't have to carry the weight of being responsible for everyone else. I could be a girl walking to school—free, even if only for a few blocks.

One morning, I was so exhausted. I had done all my chores and barely had the strength to help my younger brother and sister. I gave them a quick wash—just enough to get us all out the door in time. When I got home later that day, she asked if I had bathed them. I told her the truth: "No, Mama, I was tired." I didn't mean I neglected them—I had cleaned them up. But my words were enough to set her off.

What came next felt like punishment for simply being human. She grabbed an extension cord and whipped me without mercy. And all I could think was: If only she had stopped and talked to me. If she had explained why it mattered so much to her, maybe I would have understood. Perhaps I could've become a better version of myself. But love was never part of the correction. There was no tenderness—only pain stacked on top of pain.

She once fractured my arm. Another time, she smashed a crystal jar over my head, and I blacked out. When I finally woke up, I was lying in a pool of dried blood. My head throbbed. There was a dent in my skull. I didn't cry. I didn't scream. I just got up, took a shower, and cleaned the blood off the floor like nothing had happened. Before I could even process what I was feeling, she looked me dead in the eyes and said, "If you ever tell your father any of this, I will take care of you when he leaves." And I believed her.

At Thomas Edison Elementary, every day felt like walking into a war zone. The teasing, the stares, the whispers—it was relentless. My adoptive mother had her own ideas about fashion. She dressed me in long, outdated gowns and vintage heels like I was a character in a play set in the wrong decade. While other girls wore bright colors and fun patterns, I looked like I stepped out of an old photo album. I begged her to let me pick out my own clothes, to blend in—but she never listened. She insisted she knew best.

By the time I made it to middle school, I had built a kind of armor around myself. After everything I'd been through, I wasn't about to let anyone push me around. I stood my ground. I didn't take nonsense from anybody. School became a sanctuary—not perfect, but a break from the noise and the weight of home. It was the one place I could just be a student, not a caretaker or a victim.

Still, even there, I couldn't completely escape the ghosts. They followed me in the form of memories and hidden bruises. But I kept going. I showed up every day, even when laughter echoed behind me or when I felt like the odd girl out in vintage clothes and worn heels.

To cope, I found little ways to create joy for myself. One of them was collecting and crushing aluminum cans. Back then, you could get a penny per can. So I'd go around picking them up, crushing them one by one, until I had enough change to buy candy. Not just for me—I sold it too. Even as a kid, something inside me wanted financial freedom. I didn't know the term for it back then, but I knew I wanted to create my own way.

Even when life didn't give me much, I learned to make something out of nothing. I survived by finding purpose in the smallest things—a penny, a piece of candy, a moment of peace on a long walk to school.

By the time I turned twelve, we didn't have neighbors living right next door—just a few houses scattered about six or eight blocks away. That's how I met this one woman during our daily bus rides. We didn't talk much at first, but over time, she grew to trust me. One summer, she asked if I could babysit her two boys. I agreed, grateful for the opportunity. She paid me fifty cents an hour, and by the end of the week, I had earned a hundred dollars. But I never got to hold on to it. My mom took every cent. So, week after week, I worked—not for myself, but for her.

Middle school was no easier. The bullying resurfaced like a wound that never fully healed. I was an easy target—the dark-skinned girl in worn clothes, never quite blending in. Kids teased me for the way I looked, the way I dressed, and sometimes just for being me. But something in me had shifted. I was no longer that quiet little girl who just took it. I had learned to fight back—physically, emotionally, spiritually.

I remember a girl hit me one day over something petty. I don't even remember what it was. But something inside me snapped. I blacked out. When I came to, she was on the floor, and someone was pulling me off her. I wasn't proud of it—but from that moment on, the teasing stopped. I wasn't the girl people could pick on anymore. I had drawn a line in the sand, and they knew not to cross it.

Still, while I fought battles at school, my mother remained absent primarily from my academic life. She never attended parent-teacher conferences and never inquired about my grades. The only time she showed up was for my 6th and 12th-grade graduations—milestones that couldn't be ignored. She was like a stranger watching my life from the outside, only stepping in when it suited her image.

When I was eleven, during sixth grade, she made a decision that felt like the final blow to my self-esteem. Without warning, she cut off my long, flowing hair—hair I had cherished—and dyed it gold. I didn't recognize myself in the mirror. I looked like a stranger. And at school, it only made things worse. I became a spectacle, a target. Her choices drew attention I never asked for. And when I cried or begged her to let me look "normal," she brushed me off. My feelings didn't matter. Her vision mattered.

But even then, I refused to be crushed. I dug deep. I used the pain as fuel. I told myself, 'This will not break me.'

When I was thirteen, she let me go to a Salt-N-Pepa concert with one of my cousins. It was one of the few times I felt like a regular teenager—laughing, dancing, soaking in the music. But that joy was short-lived. As soon as I got home, the punishment came swiftly. I had forgotten to put away the food she cooked earlier that day. In my excitement and fear that she might change her mind, I rushed out of the house, not thinking twice. But for her, that was enough reason to lash out. It was always the smallest things that seemed to set her off.

But in the chaos, there was a light—my adoptive father. Daddy. He was my safe place, my favorite person in the world. He wasn't perfect, but he loved me in a way no one else did. He corrected me with kindness, guided me with love, and made me feel seen. He didn't know all the pain I was enduring, but he had this quiet goodness about him. He didn't have to say much; his presence alone made things feel better.

When I was eight, he surprised me with my first bike—just because he wanted to. He taught me how to ride, holding the seat until I found my balance. In those moments, I smiled without forcing it. I laughed without fear. He gave me little pieces of joy that I clung to like treasure.

He filled the gap left by my biological father in ways he probably never realized. He gave me gifts just because he thought of me. But his job kept him away often, and those sweet moments were always too brief. Still, they stayed with me. Every memory, every quiet act of love—etched in my heart. Christmas became my favorite time, not for the presents, but because Daddy was home. And when he was home, she—Mom—wasn't at her worst.

In the middle of all that pain, I clung to a dream—a hope. I believed my Prince Charming would one day find me. I imagined him riding through the storm, breaking through the darkness like a scene straight out of Cinderella. I told myself, One day, he'll come. He'll find my glass slipper. God will send him, and he'll love me right.

That dream kept me alive—kept me hoping—until I was fifteen when I finally left home.

With every trial, I held onto the idea that love, healing, and freedom were out there somewhere. That my story wouldn't end in pain—that it would rise, like I did, from the ashes.

LeShawn & Siblings

LeShawn & Siblings

LeShawn, Father John Edwards, & Siblings

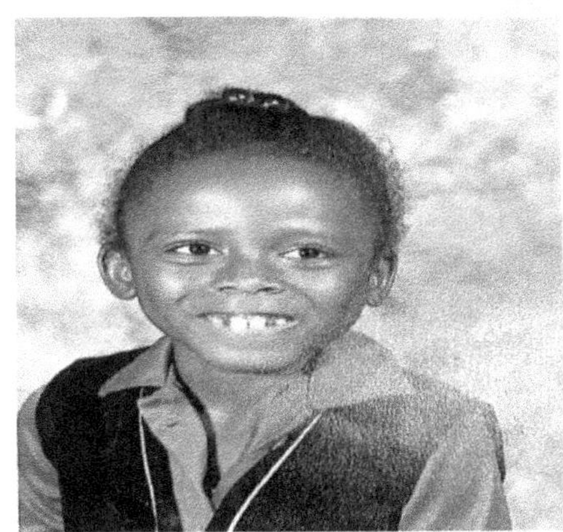

Thomas A. Edison School
Promotional Exercises
Congratulations
Class of

Mother Maybelle, Sibling & LeShawn

Adoptive Parents- John & Maybelle Edwards

Chapter Four

Becoming an Adult Child

Before I graduated from North Side High School, I attended John McDonogh—better known as John Mac. That school held some of my toughest memories. Bullying was constant, and although I often found myself the target, I didn't just endure it—I fought back not only for myself but for others who couldn't. I became a protector, but at the same time, I was always in survival mode. I fought a lot—not because I wanted to, but because I felt like I had to. It was the only way I knew to survive in a world that had already shown me too much cruelty too soon.

School became my refuge—not just from home, but from everything that haunted me. I poured myself into my academics and extracurriculars. I ran track, played softball, danced, and even took to the stage in theater and drama. I was a star in the eyes of many, but they couldn't see what was behind the curtain. Every achievement, every applause, was a form of escape. The more time I spent at school, the less I had to endure the emotional and physical torment waiting for me at home.

But even in that space of escape, the darkness still followed me. I wore my strength like armor, but underneath it all was still a girl—hurting, angry, and desperate for love. That's when he came into my life. My first love.

We met at the Catholic church when I was eleven, and he was twelve. He was kind, respectful, and so gentle—everything I didn't know I needed. At first, we were just friends. He would walk me home from church, never complaining about the distance. He made me feel seen, safe, and cared for in a way I had never experienced before.

By the time I was fifteen, our friendship had grown into something more. He became my first real relationship—my first experience of love that wasn't attached to pain. He was intelligent and dignified, attending St. Augustine, one of the most prestigious private schools in New Orleans. He treated me with honor, and I fell hard.

For once, I felt worthy. I felt like I mattered.

Then came the moment that changed everything. I found out I was pregnant. I was fifteen.

My heart sank. I was in shock. When I knew my boyfriend, and I were getting closer, and we wanted to have sex, I went to my mother and asked her about birth control. She cursed me out and told me I wouldn't be good for anything but lying on my back. I knew talking to her again was out of the question, so I went to the health department because I was old enough to sign the consent form for myself and got some birth control pills. I was shocked because I couldn't believe I got pregnant while on the pill. I wasn't ready. Later, we found out that I was given the wrong strength and the birth control pills were not going to work for me. My mother sued and won, but she never told me how much money she received. When I got older, I asked her, but she told me it was none of my business because I was a minor at the time.

I knew the moment I told my mother, it would only get worse—and I was right. Her words pierced me deeper than anything I had ever heard:

"I told you you'd be good for nothing but lying on your back."

She wanted me to quit school. She told me I'd never finish. But I made a silent vow to myself in that moment—I would finish. I would rise above her words. I wasn't what she said I was. I was better than that, and I would prove it.

I didn't tell anyone I was pregnant until I was six months along. I hid it as long as I could—partly out of fear, partly out of strategy. I knew if my mother found out early, she would do everything in her power to sabotage me. My chest had always been heavy, and it helped mask the pregnancy until my belly finally began to show.

But her instincts were sharp. She knew something was off. One day, my mother told me to go into the closet and get a dry towel for her. The towels were on a high shelf, so I had to climb on a chair to reach it. While I was trying to grab the towel, a flying cockroach landed on me. I was scared out of my mind, and I fell out of the chair, trying to get away from the cockroach. This was the day I told my mother I was pregnant because I was concerned about the baby after I fell. Her response was, "Why didn't you tell me? I could have taken you to the clinic to get an abortion!" I thank God every day that Ingrid was okay after that fall. That wasn't the only incident. There was another time when she punched me for no reason except to make me lose my baby, but through it all, Ingrid was still okay.

However, the third incident stands out as the most extreme—and it still haunts me. My mother handed me a whole bottle of citrate of magnesia, an old-school laxative, and told me to drink it. When I asked why, she said, "You need a good sh%% cleansing." I couldn't fake it or pour it out when she wasn't looking—I had to drink it right in front of her. Thank God, nothing happened to harm my baby. She made it clear: she didn't want the baby, and she didn't want to support me. Her words cut like a blade. She told me that if she had known earlier, she would've taken me straight to an abortion clinic. But by then, I had already made my decision—I was going to keep my baby, no matter what.

Despite everything, I continued attending school. I walked myself to my prenatal appointments, alone but determined. I didn't mind. I had been doing things on my own for as long as I could remember. I knew the life I was carrying was a blessing, and I refused to let her destroy the future I was determined to build. My boyfriend, the father of my child, lived far away and couldn't be there for every appointment. Still, when I think back to the early days of our relationship, I'm filled with warmth. He was patient, kind, and deeply respectful. From the beginning, he made me feel seen and safe. He took his time to learn my boundaries and understand my pain—something no one else had done.

When we finally became intimate, it wasn't just physical—it was empowering. For the first time in my life, I felt like I had control over my own body and my own choices. It wasn't something taken from me or forced upon me. It was mutual, and I felt something I had not felt before... love. I wasn't choiceless anymore.

The day I gave birth turned into a whirlwind of fear and confusion. That morning, I had a prenatal appointment, and my blood pressure was dangerously high. The doctor wanted to keep me, but I asked if I could go home to get some clothes. I told my mother what was going on, and she couldn't care less, so I grabbed a bag and took the bus to Charity Hospital. By the time I got back, my baby's heart rate was dropping, and I became hysterical. I was acting like a crazy person to the point where they had to sedate me. The doctors had to do an emergency C-section.

I remember the panic in the doctors' voices, the flashing lights, the sterile smell of the delivery room—and then nothing. I lost consciousness and slipped into a coma for three days, but again, thank God, Ingrid came out just fine.

When I woke up, the world felt different. I was told that during my unconsciousness, my mother had named my baby girl "Ingrid Olympia." That was not the name I had chosen. I had planned to name her DeShawn, a name full of personal meaning. Instead, I awoke to a child with a name I hadn't given her, a name that didn't feel like mine. It felt like something else had been stolen from me in those lost days—my voice, my choice.

My mother showed no real emotion when Ingrid was born. She paid more attention to the other women in the hospital than to me. But the moment I held my daughter, nothing else mattered. I looked into her tiny face and felt a surge of love so powerful it knocked the air from my lungs. She was my purpose now. She was the reason I would fight harder than ever before.

I went back to school with that same fire in my chest. I wasn't going to lie down and let life defeat me. I wasn't the girl she said would be suitable for nothing but lying on her back. I was more. I had dreams. I had a daughter who needed me. I was going to finish school, no matter what.

My father was initially disappointed when he found out about the pregnancy. The pain was written all over his face. But over time, he softened. He never turned his back on me. He didn't always understand my choices, but he stood by me. And when he told me that he forgave me, that he would be my support— my backbone—it made a difference to me. I felt strong. I wasn't alone.

Ingrid saved me. She slowed me down and grounded me. I stopped fighting with my fists and started fighting with my heart. I poured everything into being her mother. I wanted to be for her what I never had—steady, present, loving. The taunts, the obstacles, the exhaustion—I pushed through it all. I had no other choice.

Being a teenage mom wasn't easy. It was the hardest thing I've ever done. But I made it through school, through heartbreak, through fear. I did it for her. I dreamed of giving her the kind of life I didn't have.

When Ingrid was four, her father and I made the difficult decision to part ways. He had moved to Fort Smith, and we both knew we were young and needed time to figure ourselves out. I didn't want to wait around to see if he'd come back to me after exploring other options. I needed more. So I let go and told him we could be friends—but I no longer saw a future together.

There were too many voices in our ears—our parents, our friends—and we let them influence us. But even in separation, we found a way to work together. He respected my love and devotion to our daughter, and he agreed that she should stay with me. But my mother—Ingrid's grandmother—had other ideas. She would do anything she could to control me and get me to stay home, but I was terrified that I'd lose custody because I couldn't afford a lawyer. After I learned of the evil scheme my mother was planning; I knew I had to get out and do it quickly. See, when I ran away from home, I made her look bad, and she didn't like that, especially being questioned by my dad's family. The physical abuse was brutal. I was beaten with an extension cord, a hose pipe, and a wooden bat. I was burned with a hot pot of Gumbo that was still cooking, and she even cut me with a knife to the "white meat."

I knew there was no way I was going to be able to finish school in New Orleans after my mother sent her family to the school to harass me. So, my best friend's stepmother and father, who lived in Arkansas, took me in so I could finish school. I was only there for a short time but wasn't comfortable because I had a difficult time trusting men. I was then placed with a family who opened their doors to me out of kindness, and I was very comfortable there until their daughter moved back home. She had a problem with me from the beginning, and she didn't like that her parents opened their home to a stranger. I was still dealing with a tremendous amount of trauma from the sexual abuse on top of the physical, so I didn't trust people. It didn't take much for me to fly off the handle.

One day, after she made a comment saying she saw why I go through what I go through, I went off on her and had to leave. After that, I was placed into a group home that housed troubled teenagers and young adults. I was eventually emancipated and was released into my custody. The social workers found me income-based housing, and for the first time, I was really on my own. One of my teachers even helped me with furniture and gave me a job working at the school. This was when Ingrid's dad and I devised a plan to get Ingrid away from my mother. The plan worked, and not only did I get Ingrid, but I also got my baby sister, who was around 11 or 12.

But even as I made a life in Arkansas, something inside me whispered: this isn't the end. I knew I couldn't break free from my life of pain unless I moved forward—somewhere completely new. Even then, I knew a life in Arkansas wasn't for me. Since I was a child, I had always dreamed of Atlanta, Georgia. I didn't know why because I didn't know anyone there, but for some reason, in my heart, I felt like it was a safe haven for me. I knew what it represented: freedom for me and a fresh start.

So, I made a promise to myself—and Ingrid. We were going to Atlanta. And nothing, and no one, would stop us.

LeShawn & Ingrid

Chapter Five

You Are Not What You Were Told

As I steered the murky waters of my childhood, I often felt like I was drowning—lost in a sea of hurtful words and twisted views. My abusers used their insults like weapons, each one carefully aimed to break me down, to strip away who I was, and replace it with who they wanted me to believe I was. Their voices were loud, cruel, and persistent—determined to control my identity by boxing me into a story that never belonged to me.

But somewhere deep inside, a quiet voice whispered something different.

A flicker of hope—fragile but unyielding—kept telling me:

You are not what they say.

You are more.

I was more than their labels, more than their lies.

This chapter of my story is about reclaiming my identity—about the awakening moments that slowly peeled back the layers of pain and revealed who I truly was.

In the midst of the chaos, school became my safe haven. Within those walls, I could momentarily shrug off the heavy cloak of abuse and breathe as my true self. Surrounded by compassionate teachers and kindhearted friends, I discovered that my value didn't rest in the opinions of those who had tried to diminish me. In the classroom, I thrived. My drive to succeed wasn't just about grades—it was about proving, most importantly to myself, that I was capable. That I wasn't a failure. That I wasn't weak. That I wasn't the worthless girl they tried to make me believe I was. "That I was good for more than laying on my back!"

"I am not a failure. I am not an object of ridicule. I am not a pushover."

Extracurricular activities became another form of release. Whether I was running track or performing on stage, each victory, each round of applause, was a statement: I am here. I matter. I am becoming. Those moments helped me see joy was possible—and that I could create it. I didn't have to stay in the shadows of my past. I could step into the light.

By the time I reached high school, I started to grasp something I'd never fully known: I was worthy, my life had worth but the echoes of their words still haunted me. But I knew that if I wanted to be free, I had to challenge those lies head-on.

So, I started constantly speaking positively to myself. I was determined to be the opposite of what she said I would be. My logic was to show her better than I could tell her. I was not going to be a high school drop out, I was going to college. I wasn't going to have any more children until I was married. There were the things I would tell myself.

I wrote them. I spoke them. I prayed them. I believed them— until those truths grew louder than the lies.

Reframing my identity wasn't quick or easy. It took time, patience, and a grace I was still learning to give myself. I journaled each night, pouring my thoughts onto the page, bleeding pain into words so I could begin to understand it. Writing became a lifeline—a sacred space where I could finally be honest. It helped me trace the path from brokenness to healing. With each journal entry, I felt the weight lift just a little more.

Fighting also became an outlet—not with fists, but with fierce determination. In quiet moments, I redirected my anger and sadness and I started to realize: the power to change my life was already inside me.

And with that realization, I began choosing better. I sought out people who saw the real me—not the wounded girl, but the warrior. During this time I begin to grow and I flourished.

This has been more than a healing journey, this was a discovery of who I am.

When I became a work-in-progress

When I finally walked away from the place that had hurt me for so long, I felt a wave of relief. The air outside felt different—lighter, cleaner, like anything was possible. It was nothing like the heavy, toxic space I had come from. I had left the place, but I didn't realize I had brought the pain with me. It followed me like a shadow I couldn't shake.

I wanted freedom, and in some ways, I had it. But I couldn't run from the memories. They played in my mind over and over, like old movies that wouldn't stop. Even though I had escaped the physical space, the emotional wounds were still fresh. Every day, I was caught between dreaming of a better life and dragging around the weight of everything I had been through.

Starting over in a new place was hard. I didn't know the rules. I didn't know who I was supposed to be. Healing wasn't easy. It didn't happen all at once. Some days were better than others. Some days I could breathe a little easier. Other days, I still felt trapped by fear and sadness.

Little things would take me back—certain smells, words, or even a look from someone. Those moments made me feel like I was still stuck in the past. I felt broken, like a puzzle missing pieces, trying to figure out where I fit and who I really was.

But slowly, I began to speak. I shared parts of my story. At first, it was scary, but then I started to feel lighter. Each time

I opened up, I felt less alone. I realized that telling my truth didn't make me weak—it made me strong.

The more I talked, the more I healed. I began to see my story not just as something painful, but as proof that I had survived. That I was strong. That I had made it.

This part of my life isn't just about leaving the past behind. It's about facing it, learning from it, and choosing to grow. I've learned that healing takes time. It's messy. It's hard. But it's worth it.

I'm still healing. I'm still growing. But now, I know I'm not broken—I'm becoming.

Chapter Six

Faking It Till I Made It

I came to a deep truth one day—Arkansas just wasn't where I was meant to be.

I told my best friend Nay, who had been by my side since I was fourteen, that I believed Georgia was my way out. In 1993, I finally visited Atlanta for the first time. Something clicked. I came back the following year with Ingrid, and the second trip sealed it for me—this city felt alive with hope. Even when my dad suggested I consider New Orleans, my heart stayed focused on Georgia. He paid for a room so we could stay for a week to get a feel for it.

In 1995, after saving and planning for a long time, I finally made the move with Nay and Ingrid. I had saved $10,000—a lot of money for me back then. We also had food stamps, those old paper ones, which helped a lot while we got settled. I was nervous but also excited. I felt free like I was finally stepping into the life I dreamed of.

We moved to Hapeville, a quiet little town just outside of Atlanta. It felt like a whole different world from where I came from. As I unpacked, I thought about everything I had been through and promised myself I'd never forget my roots. But I also knew it was time to move forward.

The way I was raised left scars, but those scars made me strong. I made a promise to myself that Ingrid wouldn't go through what I did. I wanted to give her a better life—a life full of chances and dreams. I believed if I stayed focused and worked hard, I could change everything for us.

At first, we didn't have much—just the clothes we brought with us. But then, blessings started showing up. I got a job doing data entry, and a kind coworker opened her home to me, Ingrid, and Nay. It wasn't easy living with someone else, especially since she was married, but I was so grateful. Not long after, I found a program in Cobb County that offered temporary housing. It was just what we needed to start fresh.

While working at a daycare, I began to dream about opening my own. The pay was low—just $5.50 an hour—but my love for kids was worth more than any paycheck. When my boss told me I couldn't take off for Martin Luther King Jr. Day, I quit. I needed to be with my child, and no job was more important than that. This was a difficult decision because of the bond I had with the kids and their parents.

A few weeks later, my dream of starting my daycare began to come to fruition when a friend called, needing help with her kids—two small boys and a niece. I said yes. Soon, more families heard about me, and suddenly, I was making enough to move into my own apartment in Marietta, Georgia.

At first, it was just babysitting, but it grew. My apartment was full of laughter and learning. More and more parents trusted me. Eventually, I moved into a larger townhouse and converted my living room into a bright and cheerful daycare space. That little business kept growing.

By the time I was 20, I had bought my first home in Marietta and turned it into a full-time daycare. It was a huge step for me. I worked hard and started offering three shifts so I could help working parents at any time. I even bought another house nearby for me and Ingrid so the daycare could fully operate out of the first home.

But success brought jealousy. Another daycare owner didn't like how well I was doing. Then, one day, an employee left a child in a van. Thank God the child was okay, but the state took my license away. Just like that, everything I had built was gone. No internet, no social media—just me, doing all I could to figure out how to survive. I even went back to school to learn more about running a business.

My business started in 1997, and by 2001, it was gone. I felt crushed. All I kept thinking was, "What do I do now?"

To keep going, I took a job at Devereux, a place that helped troubled youth. It was tough but meaningful work. Then, one day, everything changed again. There was a fight involving 21 girls on the unit, with some trying to jump on one girl. At that time, I was the only one on-site who was experienced with working with troubled youth, so when I called for help, the rest of the staff were in a panic mold, so I got badly hurt trying to break it up. If I hadn't been there, I'm sure that girl would have been rolled out in a body bag. The nurse rushed to help me, but I didn't realize how serious it was until the doctor told me I couldn't even go back to light duty. They sent me to an orthopedic specialist, and that's when everything started to fall apart.

By 2007, I was falling and I couldn't sleep. My arm and neck were in constant pain. I had blackouts. I wasn't receiving my workers' compensation money. I had no income. The father of my children wasn't helping. Yes, I had two more girls by then. But even through the struggle, I made sure they ate—even if I didn't. I handed out brochures for a dental and medical savings plan to make a little money.

By 2008, I could barely walk. Some days, I couldn't at all. A doctor told me my body was like that of an 80-year-old. But I refused to accept that. One day, I dragged myself to the bathroom, looked in the mirror, and told myself, "Either you go get it, or it's going to get you." I wasn't going to give up.

It took time—this didn't happen overnight—but by 2011, I had started regaining some independence. I had lost my job and my health insurance. Medicaid sent a caseworker to me, and they wanted to send a nurse. I said, "If you're going to pay someone, pay Nay," because I didn't want anyone I didn't know in my house. After all I'd been through, especially with my ex, it was hard to let anyone in. I had always been strong and capable, but now I was in a situation where I needed help.

A New Path in Insurance

As I slowly started walking again and began to feel stronger, something inside me changed. I had a new sense of purpose. I knew I couldn't go back to the same old things—I wanted more for myself and my girls. I started thinking about the future, and the insurance field caught my attention. It seemed like a stable career, something I could grow in. But passing the licensing exam wasn't easy.

I prayed hard during that time, asking God to lead me. The job I had was wearing me down, especially during the holidays. I was always the one scheduled to work—every year, without fail. Management told me it was because I was the only one working hard, but that didn't feel fair. I didn't even like the job that much. It felt like I was being punished for doing what I was supposed to do. I started feeling stuck, frustrated, and ready for a change.

Then, in 2012, God made a way. I got a new job at a company called Assurant, doing data entry. I worked with Homeowners Associations, helping make sure they had the right insurance coverage. I wasn't working directly with policies, but I understood the importance of what I was doing.

The job was peaceful. No drama, no pressure. Just typing and checking records. But even in that calm, I felt like I was meant for something more. I started exploring other paths—insurance still tugged at my heart, but I also looked into medical coding, billing, and even clinical research. Insurance kept calling me back, though. I couldn't let it go.

That's when I knew: if I was going to be in this field, I was going to do it right. I would be the kind of agent who genuinely cared and helped.

Then, in May, everything shifted again. My mom had a stroke. It hit us hard. She survived, but things were never quite the same. Still, every Tuesday, she would call me.

By August, I decided to take the insurance test one more time. I told my mom during one of our Tuesday calls, and she told me, "Go for it." My mother never showed support or encouragement for anything, so when she said, "Go for it," I knew it was God.

On August 10, 2013, I sat for the exam again. I was nervous, but I gave it everything I had. The next day, I got the call that changed everything—my mom had another stroke. This one was massive. She fell into a coma, and the doctors said it wasn't looking good.

I passed the test—but she never got to hear me say it.

When I got my insurance license, I didn't just see it as a job. It felt like a promise—something sacred between me and God. I told Him, "I won't let You down." I made a vow to use what I learned to help others, especially people like my mother, who I was never able to help. I made a promise to help others— mothers, fathers, grandparents, aunts, uncles—who needed someone to honestly care when they needed insurance.

This wasn't just about selling a policy. It was about legacy.

This chapter of my life taught me that even in our toughest moments, there is purpose. That even in loss, there can be meaning. I didn't just pass a test—I rose above my past. I created a new future.

Chapter Seven

Same Men, Different Driver's License

My Journey Through Love, Pain, and Freedom

In 2004, while working at Devereux and managing the everyday chaos of life, I got married to my first husband. I was full of hope, dreaming of a life filled with love and partnership. I truly believed he was the one. I thought my love would be enough to heal his pain and help him grow. But I was wrong. I found myself stuck in a painful cycle, trying to fix someone who didn't want to be fixed.

The following year, things took a dark turn. The man I married became mentally and emotionally abusive. He stalked me, even showing up at my job to harass me. I was scared. Every day, I carried the weight of his threats. He used fear to control me, constantly warning that if I left him, he'd take our daughters and disappear to Haiti—and I'd never see them again.

But one morning, I acted like I was heading to work, but instead, I grabbed the chance to escape. I found a small house in Kennesaw where I could hide and rebuild my life. He didn't know where I was. For the first time in a long time, I felt a little safer.

Out of that marriage, I was blessed with two beautiful daughters—Miracle and Mariah, my "Double M girls." They gave me the strength to fight, to protect, and to survive. I held onto my job as long as I could until just before Mariah's birthday in June 2006. Even in fear, I found hope in freedom.

As a child, I promised myself I would never let a man hit me. I had seen too much growing up—watching my mother be abused left scars on my soul. I knew it was wrong. Even if I didn't fully understand everything then, I knew no one should ever be hurt by someone who claims to love them.

Leaving my first marriage changed me. I refused to be broken. I turned my pain into power and used it as fuel to pursue education. I didn't earn a master's, bachelor's, or PhD, but I chased knowledge. I earned certificates and associate degrees— something I could fall back on when life felt uncertain.

I'll never forget one professor, Kathryn Matthews, who believed in me when I could barely speak clearly. She never mocked me, never made me feel small. Her voice still echoes in my heart: "You can do this, LeShawn." She gave me confidence. Another professor, whose name I can't remember, saw my light after I performed a skit in her class. Her encouragement helped me believe in myself enough to double major.

At home, my daughter, Ingrid, who was only 10 at the time, and my best friend, Nay, who cared for my babies, provided me with the support I needed. With their help, I could work, study, and run my business, knowing my girls were safe.

Then came my second marriage.

This man hurt me in ways that left no bruises but broke me from the inside out. He was emotionally cruel and unpredictable. He'd disappear for days without a word, leaving me in a storm of fear and confusion. One time, he was gone for a whole week. I feared the worst. I begged him not ever to do that again. He stopped vanishing, but his emotional abuse continued.

His words cut deeper than any knife. He made me feel worthless, like nothing I did mattered. He tore down my self-esteem, little by little. I was so low, I nearly gave up. But again, my kids gave me the strength to keep going. I reached out to a holistic doctor who warned me—this toxic marriage was killing me. The stress was destroying my health.

Not long after, I had a serious health scare. My ankle swelled so badly I couldn't walk. My blood pressure shot up to 240. I could have had a stroke. The EMTs rushed me to the ER. As I sat there, scared and broken, he looked at me with cold eyes and asked, "Are you dying?" That moment told me everything. He didn't care. He might have preferred me dead than free.

I started to see things clearly. This wasn't love—it was a cycle of pain. I grew up around dysfunction, so I mistook it for normal. But God was waking me up. I prayed for the strength to leave. In 2021, when he got into trouble, I helped him—because I'm kind because I was his wife. I spent over $13,000 to protect him. And he betrayed me again.

That was it. I told God, "If You help me out of this, I'll never let it happen again. I'll never let another man lead me if it means losing myself." I decided to follow God only, no matter how long it took.

I spoke with a friend, Lo, who offered me advice from a man's perspective. I didn't want to give up on my husband, but I knew deep down things weren't right. He didn't want to work. He didn't want to grow. And then, he had the nerve to tell me I would end up like Mary J. Blige, having to pay him spousal support—$3,000 a month.

But God had other plans.

Through a miracle, I tracked his location using his email. I found out he was seeing another woman—parking his car blocks away, taking her car, pretending to be someone he wasn't. I printed photos and kept them as evidence. He thought I hired a private investigator. I didn't. It was all God.

I told him, "Sign these divorce papers or face me in court." He signed. And just like that, the other woman dropped him. I felt like I saved her from the hell I had lived through.

Even after the divorce, he refused to leave our home. His sister told me to stay, but I said, "If God gave me this house, He can bless me again. I want peace." I walked away from that house, even though the rent at my new, smaller place was the same. Peace was worth more than square footage.

Six months later, he called me.

He was homeless.

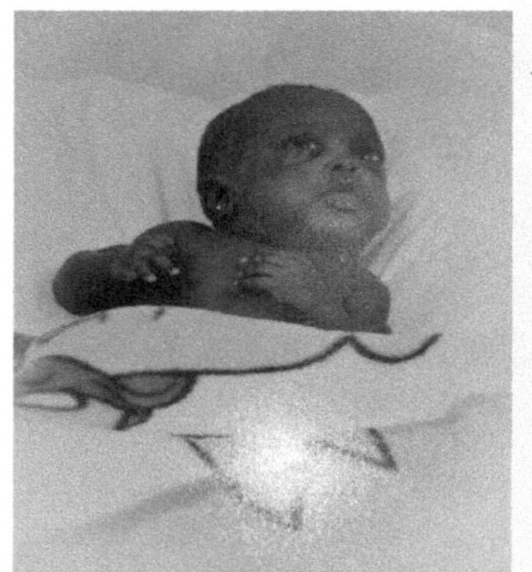

My 2ⁿᵈ daughter Miracle

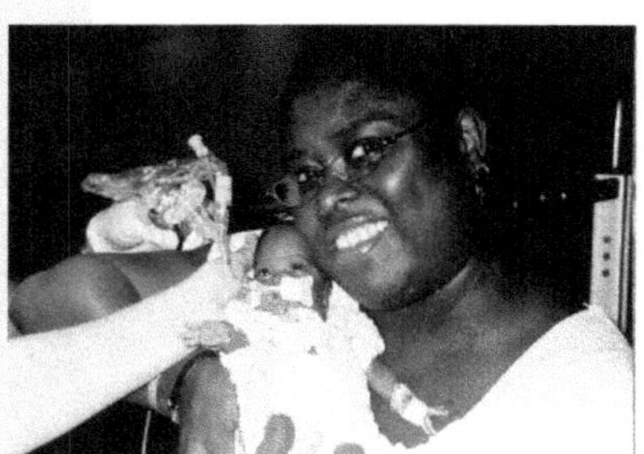

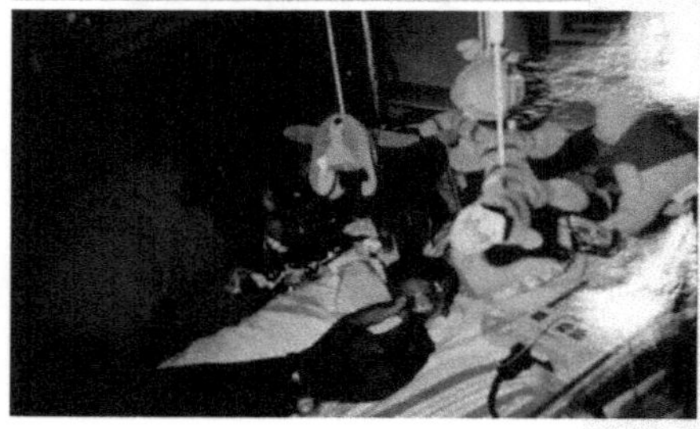

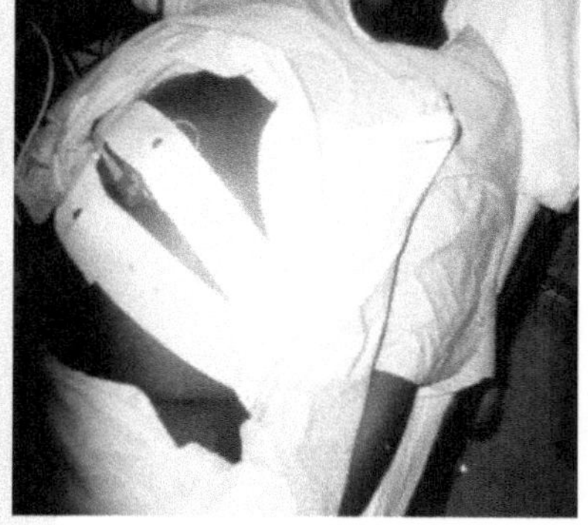

*My double M girls-
Miracle & Mariah*

Chapter Eight

Seeing Life From a Different Lens

Here I am again—paying rent, managing this small space I now call home. This is my new normal. And I won't feel sorry for myself or second-guess the choices I've made. I won't let my past decide my present or future.

One quiet evening, sitting alone, I felt that familiar pull—yearning. But along with it came a deep sense of purpose. I was determined to protect myself and my daughters. My love for Miracle and Mariah became my armor. They reminded me that I wasn't just fighting for me—I was fighting for them too. They deserved a mother who was whole, not someone barely holding it together after a broken relationship. I wanted them to see strength in me—a woman who could rise again, no matter what love tried to take from her.

Ingrid, my firstborn, is now a beautiful young woman with the most precious grandbabies I've ever seen. Their little lives are proof that something beautiful can grow from struggle. I see the same strength in Miracle and Mariah. They are graceful and confident. They don't need the approval of any man to know their worth. That's how I know I didn't fail them. I didn't rob them of their childhood the way mine was taken from me.

Still, I sometimes ask myself: Will I ever allow someone to love me again? Or will I stay locked inside the walls of my past, afraid that history might repeat itself?

As the sun set behind my new place and shadows stretched across the floor, I made a quiet promise to myself. I would take the time to heal. To find out who I am—beyond being someone's wife, beyond the pain I carried. And if love ever found me again, it would have to be on my terms, built on respect, support, and truth.

Healing became my daily routine. It wasn't just a nice idea—it became my lifeline. I started reading books about strong women who had survived heartbreak and found peace. Their stories gave me hope and showed me that I, too, could rewrite my own.

I also began journaling. Each night, I sat with my thoughts and let them spill onto the page. It felt like opening a locked door and letting light in. Writing helped me face the pain without fear or shame. With every word, I was taking back my power and shaping a new version of myself.

As I continued this journey, I found other women walking a similar path. We connected deeply, building a community that felt like home. In being open about my story—especially on social media—I touched more hearts than I expected. People began sharing their own stories with me, and I realized that healing isn't just personal—it's powerful enough to reach others.

During this season, I reconnected with God. My faith became the anchor I didn't know I needed. I had once believed that a relationship or material things could make me whole. However, I have come to realize that true peace comes from within, and it is a result of my walk with Jesus Christ. I found strength in loving myself, setting boundaries, and knowing when to say no. That was the beginning of true self-worth.

Nature became a place where I could breathe again. Long walks calmed my soul. With every step, I felt more alive. I wasn't just surviving—I was living. In those quiet moments outdoors, I chose to release the pain I'd been carrying. Letting go didn't mean forgetting; it meant giving myself the chance to grow.

Dance therapy helped me understand something lifechanging: I might not be able to change what happened to me, but I could change how I respond to it. I finally saw that other people's actions were about them—not about my value. That realization freed me from years of guilt and shame.

As I moved forward, I began to see how precious life is. Each day felt like a blank page, a chance to start again. I woke up thankful—not just for what I had—but for the lessons I had learned.

These lessons taught me how fragile life is—and how lucky I am to still be here.

So, I made another choice: to let go of resentment and free myself from the emotional grip of my exhusband. It wasn't easy—it took courage. But in doing so, I took back my power.

That night, lying in bed, I felt something new—a spark of hope. I understood that healing isn't just one big moment. It's a series of choices we make every day. I chose to forgive—not for him, but for me. I chose to believe that love could one day come back in a way that uplifted me rather than tearing me down. I chose to believe that the best part of my life wasn't behind me.

Chapter Nine

The Work

Hello LeShawn, how are you? "I just wanted to check on you because the Lord put it on my heart to pray for you."

That call came at the perfect time—like a beam of light breaking through the darkness. Just moments before, I had a painful argument with my ex-husband. He was pressuring me for intimacy, even though I knew he had been with other women. I was protecting my body, my peace, and my sanity. I wasn't willing to risk my health or fall back into the chaos he lived in.

Then he said something that shook me: "I can take it by force."

That threat sparked something deep inside me—anger, fear, and a rush of painful memories I had tried hard to forget. But it also gave me the strength to say "enough." I walked away and stepped into the quiet of my home office just as the phone rang.

It was my friend. His voice was calm, full of care. "Is everything okay?" he asked. "I woke up sweating, anxious—I've never felt that way before. God told me to call you."

At that moment, I looked up and whispered, "Thank you, Lord." That phone call saved me from falling apart. While I felt overwhelmed by fear and pressure, God reminded me that I wasn't alone.

Back in January 2022, I was still married but mentally and emotionally drained. One night, I scrolled through Facebook to escape. I laughed at funny posts and read a few articles—anything to distract myself. Then I got a message from someone I didn't know. Just one word: "Hi."

Because I work in insurance, I replied. Maybe he needed help, I thought. We had a short, casual conversation. Nothing deep. I was fragile and tired from being sick, and nothing stood out much.

In February, I saw his photo again and commented, "Nice picture." He replied with a polite "Thank you." It was simple. No flirtation. No expectations.

But then March came. And with it, something I wasn't expecting.

One evening around midnight—a time he never called—my friend rang. He'd always respected my boundaries and knew I was going through a divorce. He said he felt a heavy weight and couldn't sleep until he checked on me. That call was no coincidence. It was God showing me I was seen, loved, and protected.

As I healed, I began to recognize the patterns I needed to break. I had spent years living in "survival mode," relying heavily on my masculine energy—always on guard, always fighting to be in control.

Why? Because that's what I saw growing up. My mom dominated. I was taught to take charge or be taken over. But now, God was showing me another way.

My friend helped me step into what I call my "soft girl era." He reminded me that being a woman—being feminine—is not a weakness. It's a strength. He believes real men are meant to protect, provide, and lead with love, not control. That was new for me. I was so used to surviving that I forgot how to simply be.

I used to be defensive, always ready to clap back. But now, I've learned to listen—not to respond, but to understand. That shift has changed everything.

Today, when I have disagreements, I don't argue or fight. I communicate. If something happens between me and a friend, we talk about it. We listen. We grow through it together.

I admire his humility. He owns his mistakes. He speaks with respect. And he helped me understand that everything we do should be done in love.

God is slow to anger. He gives us grace. He waits. And I've learned to do the same. I've learned to speak with love—not in the heat of the moment, but with a calm and caring heart.

This man is my friend. I call him MY KING. He's shown me a kind of love I never knew existed. A love that doesn't hurt, doesn't take, doesn't demand. A love that respects and uplifts.

Because of him—and more importantly, because of God—I've entered a new season.

Welcome to my soft girl era. A time of peace. A time of healing. A time where I embrace the woman God created me to be.

Chapter Ten

Emergency-Answering the Call

As I reached the final chapters of this journey, I found myself reflecting on all the changes I had made. For the first time, I saw things clearly—not as I wanted them to be, but as they truly were. That clarity opened doors I never thought I could walk through. I had chosen to heal, no matter how painful the process. And during that time, I began to hear from God in a way that was both comforting and urgent.

One evening, while I was journaling in the quiet of my home, a thought came to me like a whisper: "Are you tired of running?"

It was a simple question, but it hit me hard. I realized I had spent so much of my life running from pain—covering it up with fear, staying busy, and avoiding the truth. But at that moment, something in me changed. I was ready to stop running.

A deep peace washed over me. I could feel God's presence, calling me to rise from the broken pieces of my life and step into something new. "Are you ready to obey Me?" He asked. His voice was calm but firm. And I knew it was time; time to stop surviving and start living, time to take everything I had been through and use it to help others.

That moment was my turning point.

I began to understand that my story wasn't just for me. It was meant to help someone else—to give hope to the woman who feels like she's drowning, the one who's ready to give up, or the one still hiding her pain. I felt called to speak my truth, even the parts I had once been too ashamed to say out loud.

So, I started sharing my journey on TikTok. What began as a way to release pain turned into something bigger. I talked about heartbreak, healing, and growth. I shared my ups and downs, and to my surprise, women from all walks of life began to connect with my story. They reached out, shared their own experiences, and found comfort in knowing they weren't alone.

We built a sisterhood—a community where it was safe to cry, to laugh, and to heal together. We encouraged each other, lifted one another up, and celebrated every step forward, no matter how small. I also participated in live talks and interviews, where we had genuine conversations about healing, self-love, and the process of starting over.

It was in these spaces that I found my purpose. God showed me that my pain wasn't wasted—it was preparation. I wasn't just a survivor anymore. I was becoming a vessel for healing, a voice for the voiceless, a light in the darkness.

Standing before this growing community of women, I felt nothing but gratitude. Every struggle I had gone through had led me to this place. It all mattered. And now, I could use it to make a difference.

This is my mission. My past doesn't define me. What defines me is how I choose to rise, to heal, and to share my truth with others. I am right where I'm supposed to be—and I'm walking in my purpose with open arms and a whole heart.

Chapter Eleven

Healing Never Stops

As I pause and look back on everything I've been through—the heartbreaks, the struggles, the lessons—I see how each moment has shaped me. All of it helped me grow in love, strength, and, most of all, in understanding myself.

The journey wasn't smooth. Healing didn't happen in a straight line. Some days, I felt strong. Other days, I felt like my past was too heavy to carry. The pain I held onto showed up in the way I acted and in the choices I made.

Sometimes, I reacted out of fear instead of from a place of peace. I didn't always do what was best for me because I was still holding onto old hurt. But over time, I started to recognize these patterns. And slowly, I chose to let them go.

Everything began to shift when I changed the way I saw things. I stopped waiting to "arrive" at healing and instead accepted that healing is a lifelong process. It's about learning, growing, and showing up for yourself—even on the hard days. I committed to doing the work: facing my past, understanding my triggers, and learning how to respond with grace instead of fear.

During this season of growth, I met someone who changed the way I understood love. Being with him felt like taking a deep breath after holding it in for years. He saw me—really saw me—and accepted all of me. His love was soft, patient, and steady. It helped me regain my confidence and believe in myself again. For the first time, I felt safe to be me without hiding or shrinking. His presence reminded me that love doesn't have to hurt. Love can heal.

But even with love, healing doesn't end. Life will always bring moments that trigger old wounds. That's just part of being human.

What matters is how we respond.

Here's what I've learned about navigating those moments:

1. Acknowledge Your Feelings

Let yourself feel. Don't push your emotions away. They're real, and they matter. Journaling helps me process what's really going on inside.

2. Pause Before Reacting

Take a breath. Ask yourself what the trigger is showing you. Is it fear? Is it a memory? Give yourself time to understand before responding.

3. Reach Out for Support

You don't have to go through it alone. Talk to someone you trust—a friend, family member, or even a support group. Sharing helps lighten the load.

4. Be Kind to Yourself

You're going to have tough days. That's okay. Talk to yourself with love and grace. Treat yourself like you would treat someone you care about.

5. Stay Grounded

Do things that help you feel calm and centered—like praying, meditating, walking, or simply sitting in silence. Being present helps bring clarity.

6. Remember What Matters

Keep checking in with your values. Let them guide you when you're unsure. Stay true to who you are becoming.

7. Celebrate the Small Wins

Every step forward counts. Even if it feels small, it's progress. Be proud of how far you've come.

As I close this chapter of my life, I do it with deep gratitude. Every high and low has led me here. I know there will still be hard days, but I also know I have the strength, tools, and faith to keep moving forward.

This is not the end—it's a new beginning. And I'm walking into it, healed and whole, one step at a time.

I am no longer a survivor; I am a warrior because I have survived what was meant to destroy me.

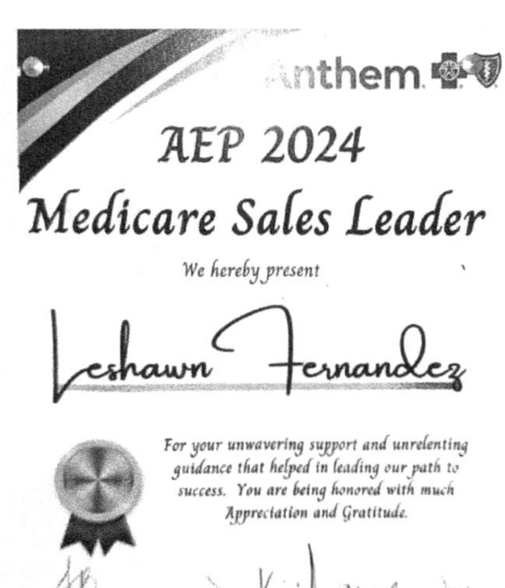
Anthem
AEP 2024
Medicare Sales Leader
We hereby present
Leshawn Fernandez
For your unwavering support and unrelenting guidance that helped in leading our path to success. You are being honored with much Appreciation and Gratitude.
JEANINE BERAM
DIRECTOR SALES
DREW KINNINGHAM
SPECIALTY SALES DIRECTOR
YVETTE WILLIS
REGIONAL SALES MGR

Anthem
2023
Medicare Sales Leader
We hereby present
Leshawn Fernandez
For your unwavering support and unrelenting guidance that helped in leading our path to success. You are being honored with much Appreciation and Gratitude.
JEANINE BERAM
DIRECTOR SALES
DREW KINNINGHAM
SPECIALTY SALES DIRECTOR
YVETTE WILLIS
REGIONAL SALES MGR

Seest thou a man diligent in his business? he shall stand before kings; he shall not stand before mean men.
Proverbs 22:29 KJV

I am a child of grace. I won my inner child battle; I am a survivor and truly blessed.

Conclusion

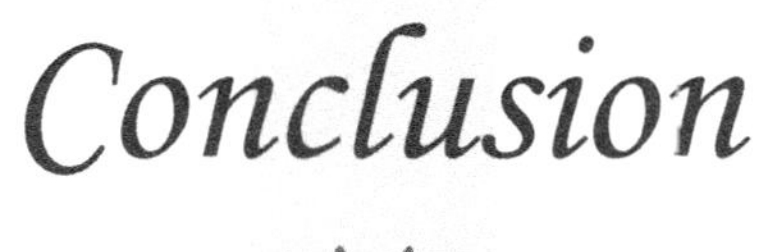

Today, I stand firmly in who I am—strong, whole, and unshaken.

Every painful moment, every step through the darkness, has led me to this place of truth. This journey hasn't been easy, but it has brought me closer to understanding my worth. I've learned how to reclaim my voice, take back my story, and wear it like a crown of strength.

Now, as you close the pages of this book, I invite you to begin your journey.

A journey of self-discovery.

Of healing.

Of truth.

Let go of the labels others have placed on you. Question the stories that no longer serve you. Your past may have shaped you, but it does not define you. There is so much more within you—strength, purpose, light.

Together, let's celebrate our identities, honor our scars, and shine without apology. Your voice matters. Your story matters. The world is waiting for your light—don't dim it.

As we continue to walk this path of healing and growth, let us remember this:

The work of healing may never fully end—but neither does our capacity to love, to rise, and to be transformed.

This is your journey. Walk it boldly. And know that you are never, ever walking alone.

Dear Readers

Thank you for walking with me through the pages of my life.

As you turn this final page, I hope you carry with you not just my story—but the courage to explore your own.

To support your journey, I created a companion workbook—a personal guide to help you dive deeper into your thoughts, memories, and emotions. Inside, you'll find prompts that invite reflection, healing, and celebration. Just as I found freedom in telling my truth, I want the same for you.

Journaling is powerful. It gives voice to what's been buried and helps us make sense of where we've been and where we're going. With every honest word you write, you move closer to healing—and to knowing yourself more fully.

So take your time. Be gentle. Be real. This is your sacred space to grow.

Grab your copy of the workbook, and start when your heart says, "I'm ready."

I believe in you.

I'm cheering for you.

And I can't wait to see the beauty that unfolds when you write your truth.

Happy journaling.

With love,
Leshawn Fernandez

About the Author

LeShawn was born and raised in New Orleans, Louisiana, and now resides in Fayetteville, Georgia, with her loving family. A proud graduate of Northside High School in Fort Smith, Arkansas—home of the Grizzly Bears—she continued her academic journey at Kennesaw State University in Kennesaw, Georgia, where she proudly represented the Owls.

Driven by a passion for personal growth and a heart for community service, LeShawn is deeply committed to inspiring her children to pursue their fullest potential, embrace healthy living, and lead with integrity. Professionally, she is a trusted and respected insurance expert, known for her dedication to excellence and service within her community.

LeShawn is also a bestselling author, celebrated for her impactful contribution to Listen Linda Presents...The Women of the Waiting Room Devotional, Volume 2. Her words continue to uplift, motivate, and offer encouragement to others walking their own journey of faith and resilience.

Connect with LeShawn at:

www.authorleshawn.com

www.hereistheinsurancelady.com